Junior High Poetry Textbook

Jess Neff

BookLeaf Publishing

India | USA | UK

Presentation by *BookLeaf Publishing*

Web: www.bookleafpub.com

E-mail: info@bookleafpub.com

ISBN: 978-93-5744-713-3

First edition 2022

ACKNOWLEDGEMENT

To my students who have inspired me to write again, and to my mother who has encouraged me to find happiness in expressing myself

PREFACE

This book is meant for anyone who is interested in traditional and nontraditional poetry alike. When Neff started teaching poetry units, it was difficult to find examples of the different types. These are meant to act as mentor or example poems for these kinds.

Quatrain - Stay Inside?

Four corners
Four lines
Four borders
Four sides

In a box
A home you have made
Your old friend knocks
Offers you aid

Beckons outside
Both go for a ride
Your mind must have lied
You should not stay inside

Diamante - Choices

Asleep
Dark Quiet
Bedding Snoring Dreaming
Deep Shallow Drowsy Alert
Sunning Playing Thinking
Bright Loud
Awake

Awake
Content Disgruntled
Planning Moving Trying
Happy Sad Good Bad
Breathing Moving Sleeping
Fitful Appeased
Asleep

Trinet - "Three Wooden Crosses"

Farm land
Raise livestock
We farm the land to feed
We raise the livestock to eat
Tractors Trucks
Buy Sell
Death Cross

Teach students
Open minds
We teach students to become better
We open minds to other possibilities
Pencils Papers
Invest Engage
Death Cross

Preach gospel
Forgive everyone
We preach the gospel to explain
We forgive everyone to bring peace
Holy Texts
Listen Understand
Death Cross

Ottava Rima - Prepping for a Trip

I must pack all my clothes in order to leave.
I must pack my toiletries for this vacay.
We will be going here soon on this eve.
We will not wait any longer to stay.
Finally we can take a much needed break,
And spend some time on the coolest, calmest
lake.

I must pack everything into the car
I must not forget even one thing at home
We all know that one person who says, "are
we there yet?" The next thing you say should be
"oome!"
Parents do not like to be pestered like that
And "Oh! Silly me! I forgot our own cat!"

Acrostic - My Dependents

Precious
Entertaining
Timid
Eager

Annoying
Noisy
Dirty

Silly
Picky
Understanding
Needy
Kind
Yeller

Reverse - Who I Am

NEFF
Teacher
Adult
Relationships
Children
90s Baby

TEACHER
Constantly Learning from self and others
Constantly Showing others what i know
Constantly Stressing over if i know
Constantly
ADULT
New Car last saturday
New House last august

Graduated College december 2016

Master's Degree

Graduated College may 2014

Undergraduate Degree

Graduated High School may 2010
RELATIONSHIPS
Family -- immediate & extended
Friends -- high school, college, adult, teacher
Significant Other -- boyfriend, engaged, break
up………...eventually
CHILDREN
Dog is Pete (5 years old: birthday october 21)

Students are Mine (since 2014) WHS mom,
aunt, sister…..

…………………………...eventually………9
0s Baby
Nostalgia
boy bands,
bright colors,
tiny braids,
flowers,
Disney,
learn to ride a pink bike with tassels

Cultural Change

NOW is phones & social media constantly

THEN was outside & free phone calls AFTER
9PM

Cinquain - Life Stages

Baby
Needy Smelly
Always crying always
Never freedom never happy
Life-Taker

Child
Nosey Smiley
Always laughing always
Never freedom never boredom
Time-Waster

Pre-Teen
Nutty Sassy
Always crying always
Never freedom never peaceful
Anger-Maker

Teenager
Noisey Scrappy
Always laughing always
Never freedom never loving
Risk-Taker

Adult
Nonstop Speedy
Sometimes laughing crying
Never freedom never fulfilled
Money-Maker

Elderly
Never Sorry
Laughing crying dreaming
Never freedom always fulfilled
Dream-Waker

Monorhyme - Releasing

Focusing on the stressing
Clearly not impressing
Fears forever pressing
Just leaves me guessing

Staring at the ceiling
Cannot fight the feeling
Thoughts send me reeling
Do not know what they are revealing

Fighting with the flowing
Cares are soon knowing
Pace is hardly slowing
Eyes started glowing

Musings of the being
Could not help but agreeing
Joys are slowly seeing
Brain is finally freeing

Free Verse - Hypothetically...

Imagine If Each Person Had One Soulmate
But You Missed Yours
Would You Be Upset?
How Would You Know?
Was It The Guy From High School Who
Graduated Early Because He Was The Bad Kid?
Was It The Girl From Facebook Who Reached
Out Because You Have Mutual Friends?
Was It The Boy You Grew Up With Even
Though You Had No Idea He Had A Crush On
You?
Was It Your Best Friend You Kissed In College
Because A Guy Dared You To?
Was It The Gender-Fluid Misfit Who Found You
As A Safe Place?
What If You Still Have Not Met "Your Person?"

What If You Missed Your Chance?
Do You Continue To Search?
Do You Go Back to Previous Relationships To
See If Maybe THIS Time Will Work?

Do You Continue To Put Yourself Out There In
The Hopes That He/She/They Will Be The One?
Do You Add More Dating Apps to Your Phone?
Do You Just Wait And See What Happens?
How Can You Continue On Like This? IT'S
EXHAUSTING!
Would You Still Look For Your One True Love?
But Maybe He/She/They Already Found
Someone Else
Imagine If You Never Found Your Soulmate

Blitz - Clearer for You

The grass is always greener,
The coast is always clearer.
Clearer than the ocean,
Clearer than the sea.
Sea as blue as sky,
Sea is a gift to see.
See the other side,
See the other coast.
Coast through life,
Coast through time.
Time is never ending,
Time is never stopping.
Stopping only to believe,
Stopping only to breathe.
Breathe through the nose,
Breathe through the tears.
Tears stain cheeks.
Tears stain sheets.
Sheets cover self,
Sheets cover mistakes.
Mistakes are meant to be made.
Mistakes aren't meant to be repeated.

Repeated loves,
Repeated losses.
Losses can be found,
Losses can be replaced.
Replaced by love and laughter,
Replaced by happiness after.
After lovers lose,
After lovers keep.
Keep in your thoughts.
Keep on your lips.
Lips meant to be kissed,
Lips meant to lie.
Lie about your truths,
Lie about your past.
Past repeats itself,
Past you must learn.
Learn from mistakes.
Learn from experiences.
Experiences make us who we are,
Experiences make us who we will be,
Be the one you wish to impress,
Be the one you wish to embrace,
Embrace the ones who love you still
Embrace the ones who support you 'til
You know who you are,
You know who you will be.
Are you?
Be you!

Etheree - Recovery

Help!
Please Help!
I'm alone,
And I cannot
Begin to believe
What will happen to me
If I keep going on like
This. I know that I need help but
Asking is such a hard thing to do.
Sometimes asking is just the first step to
Recovering from your biggest worries.
Accepting help is another thing.
Accepting help is agreeing
That something is wrong, and you
Are ready to fix it.
Sometimes you just need
A little push
To take the
First step.
Help.

Musette - Evolution of Technology

Cell Phone
Social Media
Ringtone?

TV
Disney Netflix
Judge Me?

Laptop
School at Home
Class Drop?

Haiku - Three Seasons

Summer goes away
Fall takes its place and remains
Winter sure to come

Temperatures high
Slowly settling to lower
Cold appears with snow

Sunlight shines brightly
Overcast and more foggy
Dark, little sunshine

Alouette - Cosmetic Surgery

Body Modify?
People asking why?
Breast implants, Botox, face lifts,
Changes eye color,
Always another.
Some view these all as gifts.

Easy to come by.
Some worry they will die.
Family members are miffed;
"Don't change you," says mother.
"You are perfect," says brother.
Surgery causing rifts?

Families? Some cry.
Patients? Some lie,
Trying to avoid a tiff.
Quiet is father.
Still wanting other
Procedures and lifts.

Ode - H2Ode

Water

Flowing up the beach

Falling from the sky

Rippling on a lake

Splashing from a muddy puddle

Under a child's rainboot

Rolling up the shoreline

Thundering across the night

Descending from the showerhead

Collapsing into the bay

Spiralling up into a spout

Breaking up the coast

Babbling down the brook

Dihydrogen monoxide

Brevette - Education System

Teacher
t e a c h e s
Students

Student
t a k e s
Tests

Tests
"s h o w"
Progress

Progress
"r e f l e c t s"
Skills

Ballad - Cheater, Cheater, Cursed

The woman in white
She's quite the fright.
If you're in the right,
She won't bother you tonight.

Be loyal to your S.O.
Or else, she will know.
She will take your beau
And lead him/her fro.

She will kill for the thrill
Little to no frill
Leaving bystanders ill
From seeing the body so still

Be loyal to your S.O.
Or else, she will know.
She will take your beau
And leader him/her fro.

She is just a ghost,
But she feels the need to roast
Unloyal partners without giving a toast
She need not boast. She is the most.

Alliterisen -- All Hallows Evening

Gnarly nails tap, tap, tapping.
Wind through the winding path passes through
Dark, dim, freaky forests.
Pitter patter of frantic feet;
Creepy cries fall flat.
Silence seeps uneasiness
Until midnight meets daytime.

Katauta - First Date

First Date on the mind
Getting Ready all day long
Should I wear a skirt or dress?

Clock Strikes six with no
One Here? Must be running late?
I Call. No answer. Stood up.

Cascade - Hair!

Flowing in waves down the back
Soft, sleek shining in the sun
Thin, thick, fine, coarse
Flyaways tamed with setting spray

Blonde, Brunette, Black
Natural or Wild
Purple, Rainbow, Pastel
Flowing in waves down the back

Long, cascading locks
Tight-knit curls
Edgy, pixie cut
Soft, sleek shining in the sun

Ponytails, Pigtails, Ribbons running round
Clips, Bobbie Pins, Braids
Gels, Mousses, Creams
Thin, thick, fine, coarse

Curling Iron, Straightener, Hair Dryer
Styling Wand, Hair Rollers, Brush Hair Dryer
Brushes, Combs, Picks
Flyaways tamed with setting spray

Flowing in waves down the back
Soft, sleek shining in the sun
Thin, thick, fine, coarse
Flyaways tamed with setting spray